Editing Audio Using Audacity
Second Edition
by Simon Pittman

Second edition - 2018
First edition - 2013

This book covers version 2.2.1 of Audacity. While the screenshots and examples are from the Windows version of Audacity, the steps should apply to most other systems as well.

Please note that the author is in no way associated with or part of the development of Audacity.

If you have any comments, questions or suggestions for this book, e-mail the author at **simon@libraryplayer.co.uk** or visit their website: **www.libraryplayer.co.uk**

Table of Contents

Author's Introduction

I released the first edition of this book back in 2013 – almost five years ago at the time of writing! It's amazing to think how much has changed since then, and also how much has stayed the same.

Who am I?

I'm a developer of business, audio and database applications – you can find out more about my software products (and even download trials if you want to try them) on my website at: **www.libraryplayer.co.uk**

I spent several years volunteering at a hospital radio in the early 2000s, where I had various roles and tasks (including visiting the wards, presenting, studio engineering, training, fundraising and being part of the organisations committee in various roles).

This guide to using Audacity was originally written in 2008 while volunteering, as some volunteers wished to be trained in using Audacity. When I launched my business and website in 2012, I updated the guide, and then released it as a book the following year. I've since written two more books (covering WordPress and software development)!

What's new in the second edition?

For the second edition, I've reviewed the entire book and updated the information for the most recent versions of Audacity – this includes replacing and updating most of the pictures.

How I've written this book

This book lacks technical details – it's aim is to get you started using Audacity to edit audio on your computer, and hopefully make you more confident to find out further information when required. You can also use this book as a reference, looking up appropriate sections when you get stuck.

Perhaps you have used Audacity previously, and want a refresher on how to use the software, or you've used similar editing packages, but need help getting started using Audacity. Or you could be completely new to editing audio. This book is for you!

One of the best ways to learn something is also to try it out, so I encourage you to experiment with the software alongside using this book.

How to contact me:

It would be great to hear any feedback, comments, questions or suggestions you may have about this book. My e-mail address is: **simon@libraryplayer.co.uk**

You can also connect with me on Twitter (**twitter.com/LibraryPlayer**) and Facebook (**facebook.com/LibraryPlayer**).

Anyway, enough about me, its time to start reading this book and learning to use Audacity...

Simon Pittman
11th April 2018

1. Overview

What is Audacity?

Audacity allows you to edit audio files. It is similar to other audio editing applications, including CoolEdit and Adobe Auditions, which you may have previously used.

For example, you could use Audacity to...

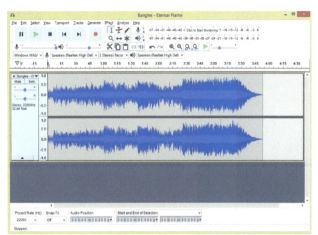

- Record and edit podcasts, radio shows and news items.

- Create and edit jingles, adverts, and pretty much any other audio.

- Convert old tapes and records to MP3 files by connecting a tape or record player to your computer.

- Edit music, e.g. to make it shorter, remove swearing, etc.

- Reverse tracks, convert music to different formats, and much more!

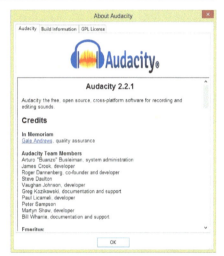

Learning to use Audacity

While the prospect of editing audio and using Audacity may at first seem daunting, it is actually very easy to use and learn. You will find that editing audio in Audacity is just as easy as editing text in Microsoft Word or editing photos in Photoshop.

This book will give you a basic overview of how to use Audacity, plus where to go to find further information. Editing audio is not scary – this book will cut out the technical details to help you get started.

You can either read this book from start to finish, or use it as a reference material, referring to particular sections and finding out about particular tasks when required. Its not designed to be a comprehensive manual, but will introduce you to all the features of Audacity, and how to use them, to help you get started using the software.

Obtaining Audacity

If it is not already available on your computer, you can obtain Audacity free of charge from:

http://www.audacityteam.org

It is available for a variety of systems, including Microsoft Windows, Linux and Apple Mac OS. While the screenshots from this book are from the Windows version, all the steps here will apply to most other systems as well.

On their website, you may see two versions of the software available – the current version, and a release candidate (which is designed to allow users to test features in the next version before an official full release) – it is best to download the latest version, as this will be more stable and reliable then the release candidate.

After downloading, you can then install Audacity on your computer.

This book will cover version 2.2.1 of Audacity – while later versions may be released after publication, most steps covered in here should still apply to future releases of Audacity.

Starting Audacity

  Once Audacity is installed on your computer, you can launch the application by going to the Windows Start menu and selecting Audacity. Alternatively you can click or double click the icon on your computer's desktop if this is available.

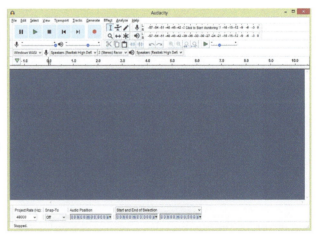

On other systems, e.g. Mac OS and Linux, the steps to starting Audacity will be different. On these systems you should be able to open Audacity using the application launcher for your system.

When Audacity starts, you will be greeted with a blank Audacity screen, ready to start a new project or open and work on an existing project or audio file.

2. Basic Features

Creating and editing audio in Audacity is similar to how you would create and edit items in other software – its as easy as editing a document in Word or editing a photo in Photoshop.

If you can't see any of the toolbars in the following sections, go to Audacity's **View** menu, and from the **Toolbars** sub-menu you can select which toolbars are visible. You can use the **Reset Toolbars** option to reset the layout and visible toolbars to Audacity's defaults.

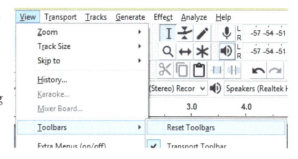

This section will cover the various buttons and options you can see in the main Audacity screen, what they do and how to use them!

Transport & Tools Toolbars

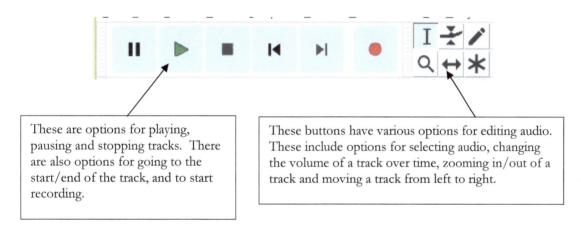

These are options for playing, pausing and stopping tracks. There are also options for going to the start/end of the track, and to start recording.

These buttons have various options for editing audio. These include options for selecting audio, changing the volume of a track over time, zooming in/out of a track and moving a track from left to right.

The buttons in the toolbar are identical and work in the same way as the buttons on your CD player (or tape recorder if you still have one!) or your audio player.

Meter Toolbars

Click the button with the microphone or speaker symbol to change options for that meter.

This includes options for changing how often the meters refresh their display, displaying the meters horizontally or vertically, and in which format the levels are displayed (either in decibels or linear).

This meter (with the microphone symbol beside it) displays the recording levels.

You can monitor the recording levels before you start recording by clicking once within this meter. Click again to stop monitoring the levels.

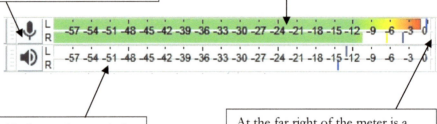

This meter (with the speaker symbol beside it) displays the levels for any audio you are currently playing in Audacity.

At the far right of the meter is a separate part of the bar, which indicates if the levels are too high. If these indicators "light up", then the levels are too high, and your audio may sound distorted.

Mixer Toolbar

This bar changes the playback volume. This bar has no effect on the actual levels of audio in your project, only on what you hear when you play back audio.

Use this bar to change the recording levels. You can monitor the recording levels using the Meter toolbar.

Device Toolbar

From this toolbar, you can select the devices used for playing back and recording audio in Audacity.

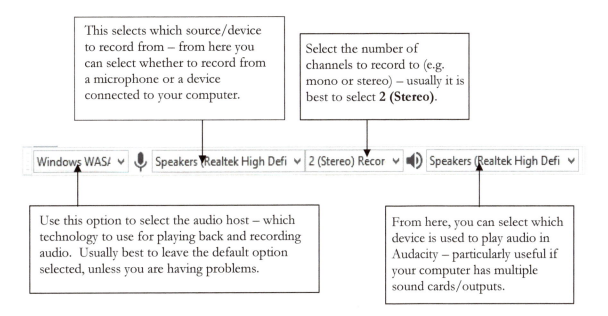

Some notes on selecting the source you wish to record from...

- **Line In** would be used if you connect a tape or record player to your computer to convert old tapes or records to MP3 files. This option should also be selected if you have connected a mixer to your computer and wish to record from this. The line in input is usually blue in the back of the computer.

- **Stereo Mix** or **Speakers** would be selected if you want to just record audio playing on your computer (e.g. an Internet clip or recording sound playing from another application).

- Select **Microphone** when you have connected a microphone directly to your computer's microphone input (usually pink on the back of the computer) and you wish to record from this.

- The names and sources available can vary depending on your computer's sound card. For example, some computers combine the Microphone/Line In input, or use different names. Select the option that best matches the above descriptions, or check the documentation for the device you are recording from, or for your sound card.

Edit Toolbar

Many of the options in this toolbar work in exactly the same way as similar options in other applications – for example copying and pasting items, undo/redo and zooming in and out. Selecting audio is the same as selecting a piece of text in Word – just drag the mouse pointer over the audio you wish to select.

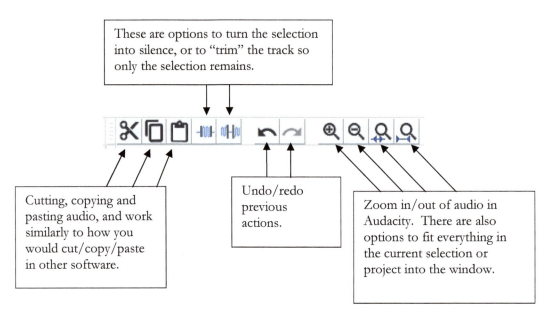

These are options to turn the selection into silence, or to "trim" the track so only the selection remains.

Cutting, copying and pasting audio, and work similarly to how you would cut/copy/paste in other software.

Undo/redo previous actions.

Zoom in/out of audio in Audacity. There are also options to fit everything in the current selection or project into the window.

Some of the above options, and additional options, are available from the **Select** and **Edit** menus in Audacity.

Moving Toolbars

At the side of each toolbar is a vertical bar. You can drag this bar to move the toolbar to a different location on the screen.

You can resize the meter toolbars by dragging the right hand side of the toolbar (or dragging and dropping the bottom right corner when the toolbar is moved).

To reset the layout and location of the toolbars in the Audacity window, go to the **View** menu, and from the **Toolbars** sub-menu select **Reset Toolbars**.

Other Areas & Sections

The small toolbar with a small version of the play button and slider next to it allows you to play the current project at a different speed (which is set by using the slider).

As well as using the options available from the toolbar, additional options are available from the menus.

Below the toolbars is a bar indicating the current position within the track.

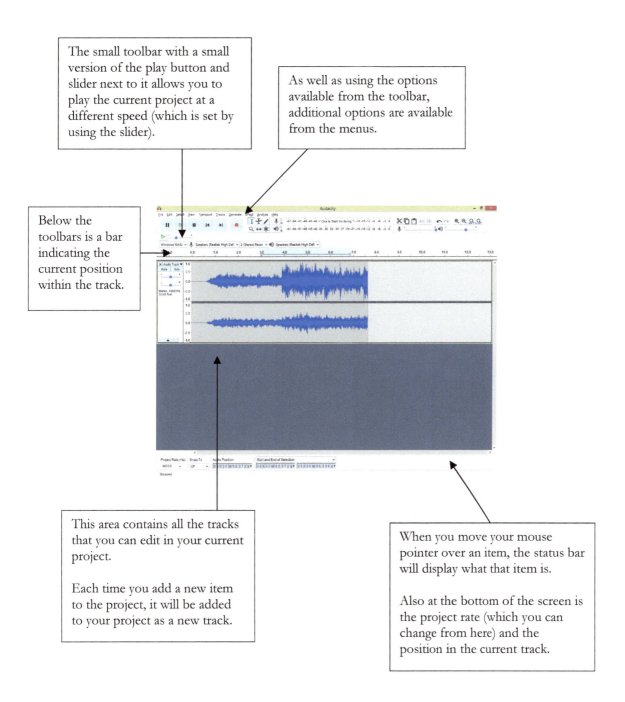

This area contains all the tracks that you can edit in your current project.

Each time you add a new item to the project, it will be added to your project as a new track.

When you move your mouse pointer over an item, the status bar will display what that item is.

Also at the bottom of the screen is the project rate (which you can change from here) and the position in the current track.

If you'd like the main Audacity window to be displayed in full screen mode – so no titlebar, operating system taskbar, etc. are visible, press the F11 key on your keyboard (and press the key again to turn off full screen mode).

Audacity Projects

When you are working in Audacity, you are working on a project. You can create a new project by going to the **File** menu and selecting **New**.

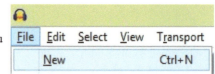

Each time you add an item (for example, by recording or by importing an existing audio file) to the project, that item is added into the project as a new, separate track.

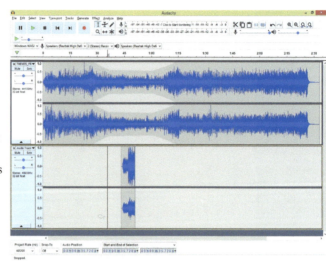

For example, if you are creating an advert for a show or podcast, you can record your speaking, that would be added to the project as a track. If you add music to be played in the background, that would then be added as a separate track. These two tracks together are the complete advert for your show.

You can edit, combine and remove tracks from the project.

When you click the Play button in Audacity, the entire project will be played.

Opening Files

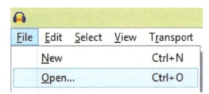

You can open a project in Audacity by going to the File menu and selecting **Open**. As well as opening an Audacity project, you can use this option to open an existing audio file (e.g. an MP3 file), which will be opened into a new project (containing only the audio file).

If you already have a project open in Audacity, when you open another project or file, it will be opened into a new window, and the original window will remain open until you close it.

3. Editing

Recording

With Audacity, you can record audio from the computer (e.g. an item playing in an audio player or an online clip), the computer's "Line In" input (e.g. if you want to record from a mixing desk or connect a tape player to the computer to convert old tapes) or any other inputs that may exist on your computer.

When you are recording in Audacity, you can still use other software on the computer (e.g. an audio player such as Library Player) without it interfering with your recording.

You may want to check the recording levels before you start recording.

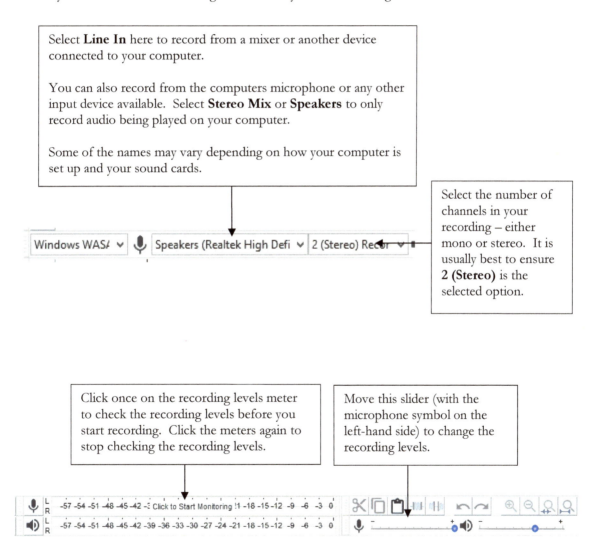

Select **Line In** here to record from a mixer or another device connected to your computer.

You can also record from the computers microphone or any other input device available. Select **Stereo Mix** or **Speakers** to only record audio being played on your computer.

Some of the names may vary depending on how your computer is set up and your sound cards.

Select the number of channels in your recording – either mono or stereo. It is usually best to ensure **2 (Stereo)** is the selected option.

Click once on the recording levels meter to check the recording levels before you start recording. Click the meters again to stop checking the recording levels.

Move this slider (with the microphone symbol on the left-hand side) to change the recording levels.

Recording in Audacity is similar to how you would record audio on a tape player, mini disc player or any other similar device! Most of the buttons and options in Audacity work in exactly the same way.

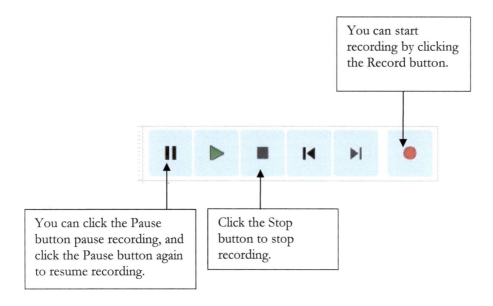

You can start recording by clicking the Record button.

You can click the Pause button pause recording, and click the Pause button again to resume recording.

Click the Stop button to stop recording.

Adding Existing Audio Into Projects

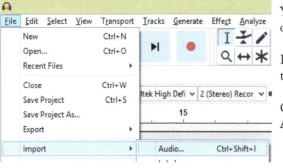

You can add existing audio file, for example an MP3 or WAV file into your project.

It will be added to your current project as a new track.

Go to the **File** menu, select **Import** and then select **Audio** from the sub-menu that appears.

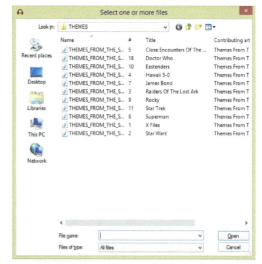

From the box that appears, you can then find and select the audio file you wish to import into your project.

Audio Tracks

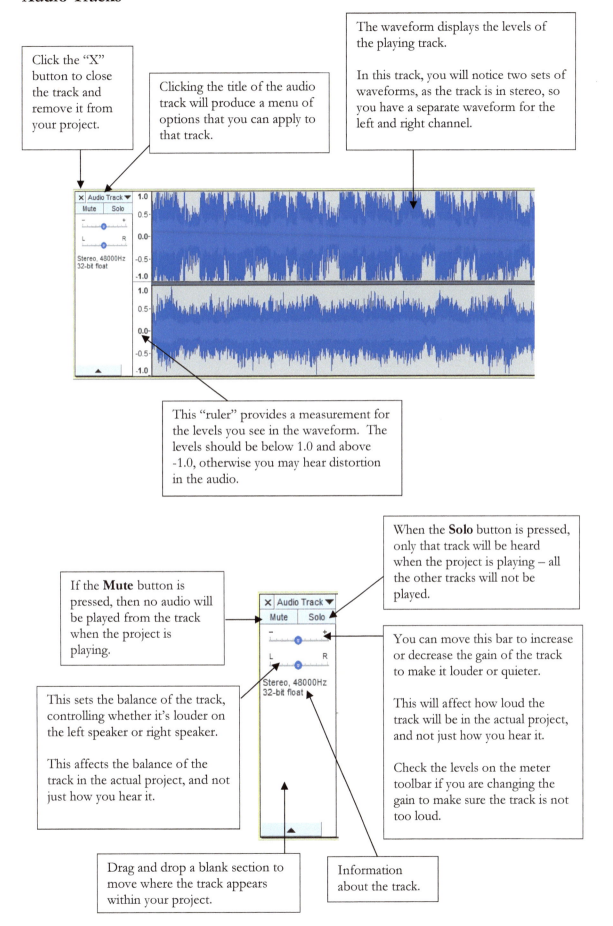

Click the "X" button to close the track and remove it from your project.

Clicking the title of the audio track will produce a menu of options that you can apply to that track.

The waveform displays the levels of the playing track.

In this track, you will notice two sets of waveforms, as the track is in stereo, so you have a separate waveform for the left and right channel.

This "ruler" provides a measurement for the levels you see in the waveform. The levels should be below 1.0 and above -1.0, otherwise you may hear distortion in the audio.

When the **Solo** button is pressed, only that track will be heard when the project is playing – all the other tracks will not be played.

If the **Mute** button is pressed, then no audio will be played from the track when the project is playing.

You can move this bar to increase or decrease the gain of the track to make it louder or quieter.

This will affect how loud the track will be in the actual project, and not just how you hear it.

Check the levels on the meter toolbar if you are changing the gain to make sure the track is not too loud.

This sets the balance of the track, controlling whether it's louder on the left speaker or right speaker.

This affects the balance of the track in the actual project, and not just how you hear it.

Drag and drop a blank section to move where the track appears within your project.

Information about the track.

To select an item in the audio track (e.g. for copying and pasting), drag the mouse pointer over the audio you wish to select. This is similar to how you would select items in other applications (e.g. part of a picture in Photoshop, or a piece of text in Word).

When you click the title of an audio track, you get a menu of options…

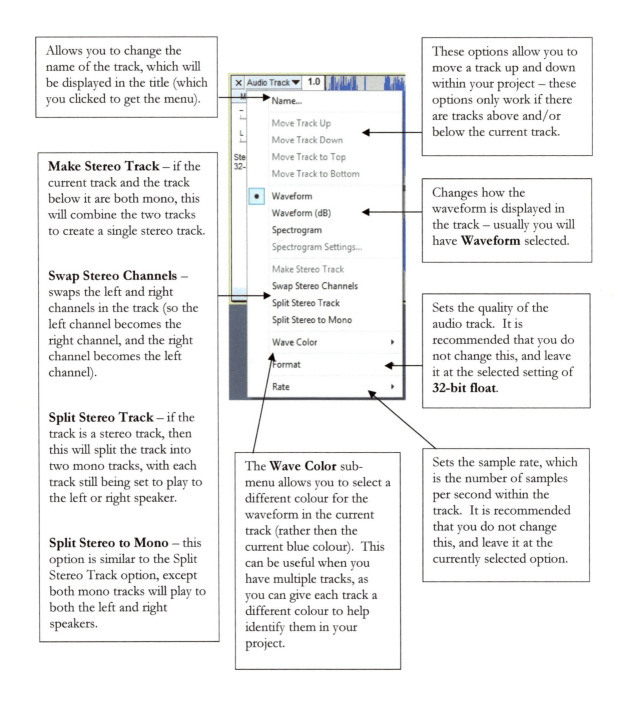

Allows you to change the name of the track, which will be displayed in the title (which you clicked to get the menu).

These options allow you to move a track up and down within your project – these options only work if there are tracks above and/or below the current track.

Make Stereo Track – if the current track and the track below it are both mono, this will combine the two tracks to create a single stereo track.

Swap Stereo Channels – swaps the left and right channels in the track (so the left channel becomes the right channel, and the right channel becomes the left channel).

Split Stereo Track – if the track is a stereo track, then this will split the track into two mono tracks, with each track still being set to play to the left or right speaker.

Split Stereo to Mono – this option is similar to the Split Stereo Track option, except both mono tracks will play to both the left and right speakers.

Changes how the waveform is displayed in the track – usually you will have **Waveform** selected.

Sets the quality of the audio track. It is recommended that you do not change this, and leave it at the selected setting of **32-bit float**.

The **Wave Color** sub-menu allows you to select a different colour for the waveform in the current track (rather then the current blue colour). This can be useful when you have multiple tracks, as you can give each track a different colour to help identify them in your project.

Sets the sample rate, which is the number of samples per second within the track. It is recommended that you do not change this, and leave it at the currently selected option.

Moving Audio Around Using The Time Shift Tool

The time shift tool allows you to move a track from left to right, to set when the track starts within your project.

For example, if you create an advert, and you have a track containing speaking and a track containing background music, you can use the time shift tool to move the speaking track, so it starts a few seconds after the music.

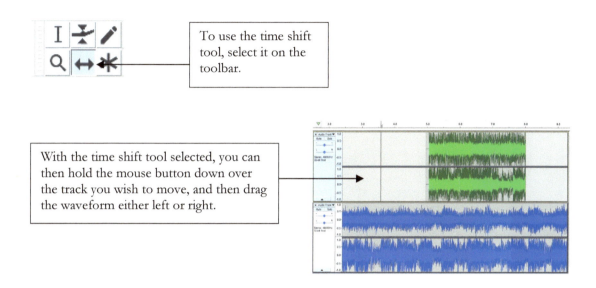

To use the time shift tool, select it on the toolbar.

With the time shift tool selected, you can then hold the mouse button down over the track you wish to move, and then drag the waveform either left or right.

Using The Envelope Tool

The Envelope tool can change the volume of a track gradually over time. For example, if you are recording an advert, you can use this facility to fade down the background music when the speaking starts, and then fade up the music again when the speaking stops.

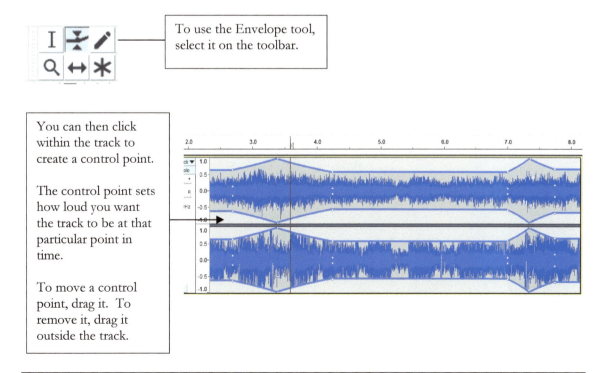

To use the Envelope tool, select it on the toolbar.

You can then click within the track to create a control point.

The control point sets how loud you want the track to be at that particular point in time.

To move a control point, drag it. To remove it, drag it outside the track.

Edit Menu

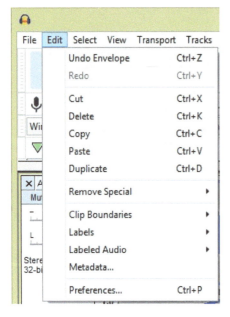

The Edit menu has a range of additional editing options. Some of the options in the menu are also available from the various toolbars covered in previous sections.

Undo and **Redo** allow you to undo or redo previous actions.

Cut, **Copy** and **Paste** allow you to cut, copy and paste audio in Audacity, and work similarly to the cut / copy / paste options that you find in other software.

Delete removes the selected audio from the track.

Duplicate – copies the current selection to a new track.

The **Remove Special** sub-menu includes options to cut or delete the current selection (leaving blank/silent audio where the current selection is), convert the selected audio into silence, and to trim/delete everything in the current track that is not selected.

The **Clip Boundaries** option allows you to split the current track into different clips/sections.

The **Labels** and **Labeled Audio** sub-menus include options for adding and editing labels within your project – labels are short notes that you can include in your project, and labels are displayed in the Audacity window as a separate track (containing text labels rather then audio). Labels are covered in more detail later on in this book.

From the **Metadata** option you can edit the track information for the current project, for example ID3v1 and ID3v2, containing the artist, track title, year, etc. This information will be included in any audio files you export. This is the track information you see in audio players.

Preferences allows you to change the settings in Audacity, this is covered in a later section. If you use Audacity within your workplace chances are you will not need (and should not) touch anything in the preferences.

Effect Menu

There are a range of effects available from the Effects menu.

For example, you can amplify your audio to make it louder, create a "fade in" or "fade out" effect. The best way to become familiar with these effects is to experiment with them yourself.

Some options/effects are obvious, while other names may not make much sense to those unfamiliar with editing audio - and even those with years of experience editing audio may be unfamiliar with some of the options!

To use any of the effects, first select the audio you want to apply the effects to, and then select the effect you want from the menu.

You may get a series of options that apply to that effect, or the effect will be applied straight away.

It is also possible to download and install additional effects within the software – further information on how to do this is available from Audacity's web site.

Try experimenting with the different effects – chances are there are many effects you may never use, but there are other effects that you could find useful in the future.

It can be great fun hearing what the different effects can do to your audio!

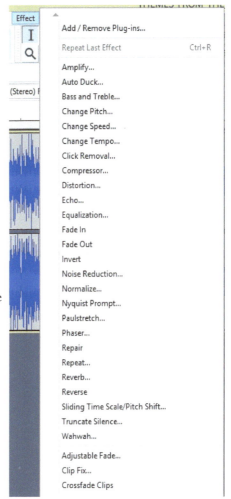

4. Saving Work

How Audacity Saves Files

When Audacity saves a project, it creates a project file, and then a series of small audio files in a folder with the same name as your project. For example, if you save your project as **Example**, there will be a project file called **Example**, and in the same folder as the file, there will also be a folder called **Example_data**.

Example_da ta   Example

This allows Audacity to open its project files quickly.

Make sure you do not delete or move the project file or folder.

Audacity projects can only be opened in Audacity, and can not be opened in any other audio application. Once you have completed your project, you will need to export your project to either an MP3, WMA or WAV file.

Saving a Project

To save a project in Audacity, go to the **File** menu and select **Save Project As**.

In future, when you want to save your project, you can then just select **Save Project** from the **File** menu.

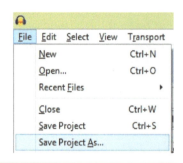

You may then see a warning advising you how Audacity saves projects. If you see this message, click the **OK** button.

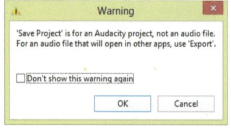

You can then select the folder where you wish to save your project and to enter a filename.

If you use Audacity within your workplace, make sure you save your files in the folder you are meant to save it to!

Saving & Exporting to Audio Files

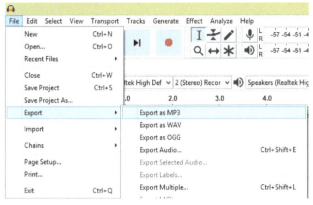

When you have completed your project, you will want to export your project as an MP3 or WAV file, so that it can be used and played in other software.

It is recommended that you export your project as an MP3 file, as this takes up significantly less disk space then WAV files, and is a widely supported file format.

To export your project as an MP3 file, go to the **File** menu, select **Export** and then select **Export as MP3**.

You can then select where you want to save your MP3 file to, and enter a filename.

At the bottom you can select the bit rate – the higher the bit rate, the higher the quality of your MP3 file – although the higher the bit rate, the larger file will be as well. You may wish to spend some time experimenting with the different bit rates, and seeing which options work best for you.

It is best to leave **Preset** selected, and set the **Quality** to **Standard, 170-210 kbps**.

Or if you'd rather use the **Constant** bit rate option – 160kbps is the best option to select – you'll get a high quality, with a good file size.

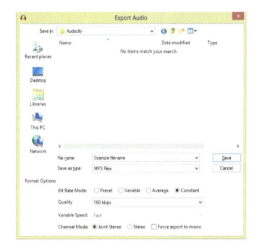

You will be asked to edit the metadata tags – this is the ID3 information that will be stored within an MP3 file. This is the information your audio player uses to retrieve and display track information, for example the artist name, album and year.

You can either enter the information, or leave all the details blank and click **OK**.

This will create an MP3 file, which can then be played in other software, for example Windows Media Player or Library Player.

Export Multiple

This option allows you to export each individual track or label in your project as separate audio files.

You can access this option by going to the **File** menu, selecting **Export** and then selecting **Export Multiple**.

For example, if you have converted vinyl or tape and have separated the different songs, you can use this option to save them to separate audio files.

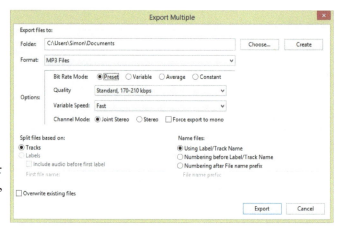

Additional Export Options

When you go to the **Export** section in the **File** menu you will notice various other options for exporting your audio – some of the options that may be of interest include…

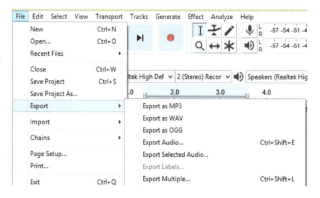

Export as WAV – this will export the current project as a WAV file – although widely supported by many audio players, these files can be very large, as there is no compression.

Export as OGG – export your project as an Ogg Vorbis format. This is a file format similar to MP3, however not all software can read this type of file, so you may not wish to use this format.

Export Audio – similar to the above options, except you will need to select the file type from the **Save as type** option. The only difference between this option and the previous option is that the file type was selected for you to reflect the appropriate option. As well as the previously mentioned formats, additional file formats are available, for example WMA.

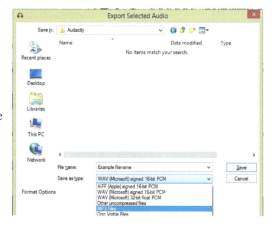

Export Selected Audio - only export the audio that is currently selected.

Export Label - export your labels as text files. For example, if you are using Audacity to convert tracks on tapes or records to digital audio, you can use the labels in Audacity to mark the start of each track, and then use this option to export a list of tracks. Labels are covered in the next chapter of this book.

5. Additional Features

The additional features in this section will only be covered briefly – these are more advanced features, and hopefully this section can get you started, and then you can read Audacity's help file/manual if you would like further information.

Labels

Labels work in a similar way to audio tracks. However, rather then containing audio, they contain text.

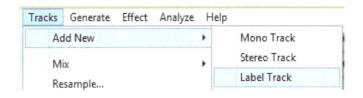

You can use labels to label items in your project, e.g. to mark where certain items start within a recording, or where each song is when converting old tapes to MP3 files.

Labels have no effect on how your project will sound, and are designed to allow you to add text and comments that may be helpful while working on your project.

You can have more then one label track within your project.

To create a new label track, go to the **Tracks** menu, select **Add New** and then select **Label Track**.

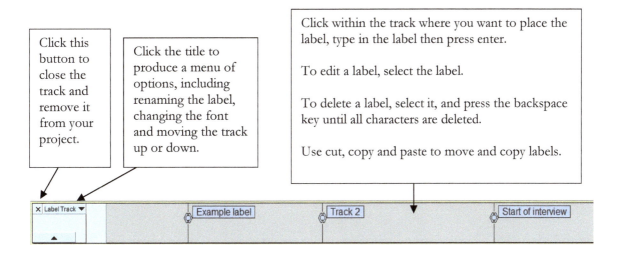

Click this button to close the track and remove it from your project.

Click the title to produce a menu of options, including renaming the label, changing the font and moving the track up or down.

Click within the track where you want to place the label, type in the label then press enter.

To edit a label, select the label.

To delete a label, select it, and press the backspace key until all characters are deleted.

Use cut, copy and paste to move and copy labels.

Additional options for labels are available by going to the **Edit** menu and selecting **Labels** – this sub-menu includes options for adding labels for the currently selected item in your audio and pasting text into a new label. From the **Edit** menu you will also find the **Labeled Audio** sub-menu, which includes options for editing the audio connected to the currently selected label.

Time Tracks

A time track allows you to change the speed of all audio within your project. You can only have one time track within a project.

To create a time track, go to the **Tracks** menu, select **Add New** and then select **Time Track**.

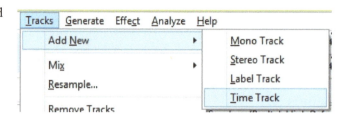

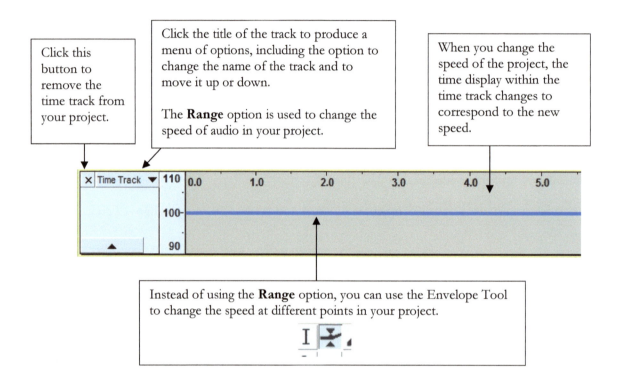

Click this button to remove the time track from your project.

Click the title of the track to produce a menu of options, including the option to change the name of the track and to move it up or down.

The **Range** option is used to change the speed of audio in your project.

When you change the speed of the project, the time display within the time track changes to correspond to the new speed.

Instead of using the **Range** option, you can use the Envelope Tool to change the speed at different points in your project.

Menu Options

The **Select** menu includes options for selecting items within your project, including selecting all items.

The **View** menu includes options for zooming in and out (some of these options are available in the toolbars covered earlier in this book), and selecting which toolbars are visible. The **History** option in the **View** menu can be useful for seeing previous actions you have carried out in Audacity.

There are a range of other options available from the menus that are not covered in this book – most of these options contain more advanced options for editing and your projects, or are options that are available in the toolbars or tracks that have already been covered in this book.

If you want to find about these menus and options, you can look them up in the help file.

6. Audacity's Settings

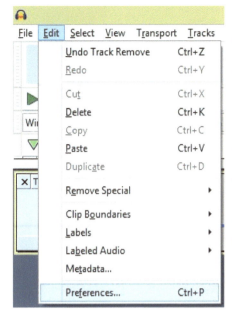

You will not usually need to change any of Audacity's settings, especially if you are using it within your workplace, voluntary organization, etc. as it will already be set up. If you do make any changes within your workplace, remember to check with your IT or Technical manager first!

This book will only cover the settings you will usually need to change when setting up Audacity. If you do not know what a setting does, don't change it! You may also want to take a note of any settings you change.

To access Audacity's settings, go to the **Edit** menu and select **Preferences**.

At the bottom of the settings, you can click **OK** to save and apply any changes you made, or **Cancel** to close the settings without making any changes. There is also a button to display help and information on the current section within the settings.

Devices

This section allows you to select the sound cards you will use.

If you have more then one sound card on your computer, you can select which sound cards to use for playback and recording.

More importantly, you can set the number of channels. The best option to select here is **2 (Stereo)**.

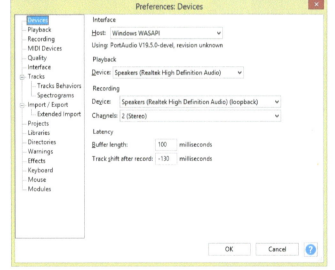

Recording

These are options for recording audio – they are worth checking over to make sure Audacity behaves as expected while recording – if you encounter any problems while recording it is worth looking at the options in this section.

With the **Other tracks while recording (overdub)** option selected, when you record an item into a new track, any items that are in the other tracks at that position will play while recording. While this option could be useful if you are voicing over some music, you may wish to unselect this option (especially if you experience feedback while recording).

When you click the record button, Audacity will record onto the current track, unless you select the **Always record on a new track** option.

Import / Export

Under the Import / Export section you can set the options for exporting/saving to various different types of files.

You can also select whether to make a copy of uncompressed audio that is being imported or to read the original file. The best option to select is **Copy uncompressed file into the project**.

You can set the quality and bit rate of exported audio files when you export the files (these will appear in the "Format Options" section when you are selecting a location, file name and file type for your exported file).

Depending on which file type you select, the option to set the metadata information (the track information, e.g. year, album, etc. that appear in your audio players) – you can either enter the information, or just leave it blank, and click **OK** to continue.

Adding support for MP3 files

To be able to export/save MP3 files, you need to download a separate file, **lame_enc.dll** – the reason for this is that different countries have different laws regarding MP3 files and copyright.

When you attempt to export a file as an MP3 for the first time, you may be prompted to download the file.

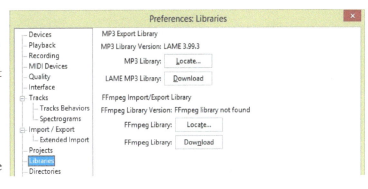

This is probably the part of setting up Audacity that most people find difficult – and puts some people off using Audacity. However, setting up support for MP3 files is really quick and simple – and you'll only need to carry out these steps once (after you install Audacity).

1) Download the **lame_enc.dll** file if you don't already have it on your computer (there are links on the download section on Audacity's website at **www.audacityteam.org**) and install.

2) Go to the **Libraries** section of Audacity's settings.

3) In the **MP3 Export Library** section, click the **Locate** button for the MP3 Library option.

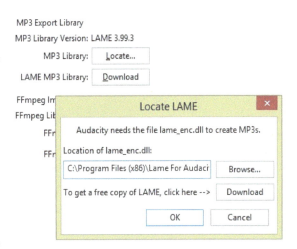

4) From the window that appears, you can locate the lame_enc.dll file that you installed – there is also a link to download if you haven't yet installed it. Click the **OK** button.

5) Once you have done this, you will then be able to export your Audacity projects as MP3 files.

Interface

From the **Interface** section you can set various options related to the display of the application.

Most of these are self explanatory (and if you don't know what the option does, usually its best not to touch it).

The **Location of Manual** option allows you to set where

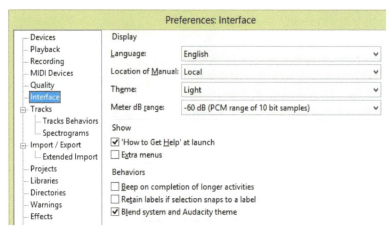

Audacity looks for its help file – it can either use the copy of the help installed with the application (the default option, and its best to leave this one selected) or to go online and access the manual from the developer's website each time you access the help.

The **Theme** option allows you to customise how Audacity appears and looks – the "Light" theme is the default theme. There is also a "Classic" theme (pictured) you can select if you prefer the look and feel of earlier versions of Audacity. The "Dark" theme is also worth a look!

The **How to Get Help at Launch** option can be selected if you'd like Audacity to display links to its various help and documentation at startup – this is particularly useful for those new to using the application.

The **Extra menus** option displays additional menus in Audacity's titlebar – however most of the options in these menus are already available in the toolbars and elsewhere.

Keyboard & Mouse

The **Keyboard** settings allow you to set up different keyboard shortcut keys. The **Mouse** section allows you to set up different behaviours and commands for your mouse.

Other Settings

Many of the more advanced settings are not covered in this book – you can look up these options in Audacity's help if you are interested in investigating further!

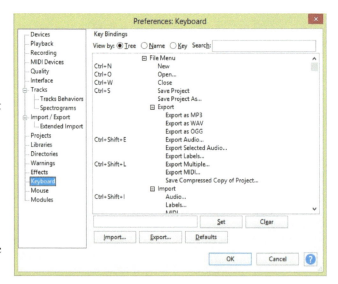

7. Further Information

One of the best ways to become more familiar with Audacity is to experiment and try and use the different options and features for yourself. Hopefully this book has provided you with a good starting point, and you are now more confident using Audacity to edit your audio.

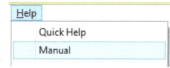

This section will cover further resources and help available.

Help File

From Audacity's **Help** menu you will see two options for help – the **Quick Help** option displays a simple "getting started" guide, while the **Manual** option displays much more detailed help on using Audacity and the different features.

Unlike documentation provided with most other software, Audacity's help file explains its features and how to use them clearly so that even someone with little IT or audio editing skills can understand them.

If either the getting started guide or manual are not included in your installation of Audacity, you can view them online at **www.audacityteam.org**

Each time you start Audacity, you may see a screen with links to their help file and manual, plus additional resources including their forum and wiki.

Within Your Own Organisation

If you use Audacity at your workplace or voluntary organisation, your IT or Technical manager may be able to provide you with further training or help.

Online

If you search online – you may find YouTube videos explaining and guiding you through the different features of Audacity – there are also online forums, groups, etc. you can join to ask for help. A great place to start is Audacity's website, which includes the documentation mentioned above, plus additional resources.

Need help editing your audio?

If you would like help editing your audio files and recordings, or you don't have time to edit the files yourself, I am happy to consider freelance opportunities for audio editing. To discuss further, send me an e-mail at: **simon@libraryplayer.co.uk**

Also by the author

Managing a WordPress Website

2016 (Second Edition)

If you are responsible for the day to day management and updating of a WordPress website, this book will help you learn and use the different features you need. With less technical detail and more emphasis on managing an existing WordPress website, this book covers editing pages, posting blogs, keeping the WordPress software up-to-date and much more! Originally published in 2014, an updated second edition was made available in 2016.

How to Develop Software

2015

Whether you are interested in learning about how software is developed or interested in a career, this book will help you get started. Illustrated with examples, and using a language with English-style statements, this book will help you start to understand the concepts and ideas involved with developing software and coding.

www.ingramcontent.com/pod-product-compliance
Lightning Source LLC
Chambersburg PA
CBHW050935060326

40690CB00039B/533